HAMSTERS

Junior Petkeeper W9-ARC-999

Fiona Henrie

Consultant Editor
Michael Findlay M.R.C.V.S.

Photographs by Marc Henrie A.S.C.

Franklin Watts
London New York Sydney Toronto 1980

Franklin Watts Limited
8 Cork Street
London W1

© 1980 Franklin Watts Limited

SBN UK edition: 85166 858 5
SBN US edition: 531 04186 7
Library of Congress Catalog Card No: 80 50483

Phototypeset by Tradespools Limited, Frome, Somerset
Printed in Great Britain by
Tindal Press, Chelmsford, Essex

The publisher and author would like to thank the following
for their help in preparing this book: Xenier Mawby; National Hamster Council

Contents

Proper food and care will help keep your hamster in good condition.

Introduction

Hamsters are live animals, not toys. They can feel hot or cold, hungry or satisfied. They can feel afraid or safe, comfortable or in pain.

A hamster needs to be looked after all the time. It will cost extra money each week to feed and care for your pet.

You will need your parents' permission to have a hamster as you may need their help to look after it. Hamsters may live to be two or three years old.

Hamsters are interesting pets to care for, and perhaps to show. If you become a responsible pet owner, you will have an attractive and lovable pet.

Note to parents

If you decide to have a hamster in your household, please be quite sure that it is wanted by you, your child and your family, and that the interest will not wear off after the first few weeks. You must be sure that you are willing to supervise its care and well being, and to cover the cost of its upkeep for two or three years. It would be unfair to the animal, to you, your child and your family to become unwilling pet owners.

If you buy a hamster from a breeder, there will be many different kinds to choose from.

When choosing a hamster, see that its body feels firm and its coat is smooth and shiny. Avoid hamsters which hide in corners or try to bite.

Choosing a hamster

It is best to buy a pet hamster when it is about five weeks old. Perhaps you know a pet owner whose female hamster has had a litter (young). Schools which keep hamsters may have young for sale.

You can also buy hamsters from a pet store or a hamster breeder. If you go to a pet store, be sure that it is a clean place with a good reputation for healthy animals.

You must be sure that the hamster you choose is healthy. It should have a thick, smooth, silky coat. There should not be any bare patches, cuts or wounds in its skin.

The hamster's body should be firm

6

The breeder will put the hamster on a special frame so that you can look at the animal more closely.

and well rounded. It should be able to stand on all four legs, and walk and run easily. Do not choose a hamster which hides away in a corner or one which tries to bite.

Its eyes should be bright and clear, not dull or running. The ears, nose and mouth should be clean, and free from any discharge. Its breathing must be even and quiet.

If you buy a hamster from a shop, you may not know where it originally came from. You must know this if you want to breed pedigree hamsters.

If you are unsure about which sort of hamster to choose, visit a show where many kinds of hamsters are exhibited.

Hamster living in a plastic tank. When you fix the water bottle to the cover of the tank, see that the hamster can reach the spout easily. Also check that the cover is well ventilated.

Preparing for your hamster

Before you collect your hamster, get all the things in advance which it will require. You will need to buy a suitable cage from a pet shop or a store. The cage should be made of metal or plastic, with a tightly-fitting lid. Do not use a wooden cage unless it is lined with metal. Hamsters can easily gnaw through wood. The cage must be strong, dry, secure and large enough for the hamster to move around in.

A good cage size for a hamster is 60 × 30 × 23 cm (24 × 12 × 9 in). The more space the hamster has to move around in the better. Do not buy

anything smaller than 45 × 25 × 30 cm (18 × 10 × 12 in).

The hamster will need a small dish for food, and a gravity-flow bottle for drinking water. Buy enough food for the first few days.

You will need some covering for the floor of the cage. You can use sawdust, wood shavings, peat, or cat litter. The hamster will need some hay or special vegetable parchment shredded up for its bedding.

Your hamster will also need a small block of hard wood to gnaw on, and an exercise wheel to play in. You will be able to buy all these things at a pet store.

Bring your hamster home in its cage or in a strong, dry box. Return home quickly so as to disturb the hamster as little as possible. Remember to keep the box or cage level.

Taking your hamster home

When you go to collect your hamster, take the cage or a roomy, dry container, such as a cake tin, to carry it home.

Punch some air holes near the top of the container, so that the hamster can breathe. If you use a cake tin, see there are no sharp points that might hurt the hamster. Put some fresh hay and a little food – nuts or bits of fruit or vegetable – on the bottom of the box.

Find out the sex and age of the hamster, and what foods it is used to.

When you arrive home, place the

When putting the hamster into its new home, give it time to settle in. Handle it as little as possible during the first couple of days.

cage in a warm place away from doors or windows. Put the cage on a shelf or table, but not on a window ledge or anywhere which is in direct sunlight.

If your cage is an open one, put extra bedding inside to keep the hamster warm. A tin can (see there are no sharp edges) or a dark glass jar will make warm sleeping places.

If the hamster is going to live outside, put the cage in an insulated shed. Do not put the cage on or near the floor where it is very cold, or where other animals can reach it.

Above left
You can buy hamster food mix in large bags. As the food is dry, it will last a long time. Wash the food dish in hot water every day.

Above right
Give the hamster some fresh green food every day. A lettuce leaf is sufficient. The best time to feed a hamster is in the evening.

Food

Hamsters need a varied diet to keep healthy. They eat cereals, fruit, vegetables, nuts, seeds and green plants. You can buy pellet foods and seed mixes which are made specially for hamsters.

Hamsters need to have clean, fresh water to drink at all times. You can use a water bowl, but the water will get dirty very quickly.

A gravity-flow water bottle has a spout which curves through the bars of the cage. The spout should be low enough for the hamster to reach easily. The spout must not be so low that it touches the floor of the cage, as the water will drain away.

12

A hamster uses its two front paws to hold its food. Hamsters need a varied diet, and they are very fond of peanuts.

Your hamster needs only a tablespoonful of cereal each day. Cereal can be given dry or mixed with a little water to make a crumbly mixture.

Give your hamster fruit and vegetables (but not onions or citrus fruits) cut into small pieces. Hamsters also like to eat bird seed and sunflower seeds. Other foods hamsters like are hard-boiled eggs, cheese, tiny pieces of flaked fish (see that all bones are removed) or cooked lean meat. You can also give plants such as dandelion and clover.

Some plants are poisonous to hamsters, so only give plants which you know are safe.

Hamsters do not always eat immediately. They have pouches in each cheek, in which they carry food. They unload the pouched food in a storage place. Later they go to this place and eat some of the food. This photograph shows a hamster with full pouches.

Hygiene

Hamsters usually use one corner of their cage for their toilet. Put a layer of sawdust, peat or cat litter on to the floor of the cage to soak up any dampness and droppings. Hamster droppings look like small brown pellets. They will be firm if the animal is healthy.

When you know the place the hamster uses for its toilet, put a small tray or lid under the litter. Take out the tray with the damp litter and droppings every day.

If the cage, especially the toilet area,

When you clean the hamster's cage, make sure that the hamster is in a safe place. Give it some food and a toy to keep it amused.

is kept clean there will be no bad smells.
Clean the cage out completely once a
week. A cage with a mother and her
young needs to be cleaned out daily.

Put the old food and dirty litter into a piece of newspaper and throw it away.

Before you clean the cage, take out
the hamster and put it in a safe place.
If you have a plastic cage with a
removable wire top, put the hamster
under the top on some paper. Give the
hamster some food while you clean
the cage.

Remove the food bowl, uneaten wet
food and the water bottle. Take out all
soiled bedding and litter, and throw it
away.

15

Sometimes bits of litter get stuck to the side of the cage. Clean out awkward corners with an old knife or spoon.

Wash the cage with hot water and disinfectant. Check that the disinfectant is safe for animals. Rinse the cage very carefully and dry it thoroughly. You can dry the cage on top of a radiator or in a low oven. A hamster living in a damp cage might catch a cold, or even pneumonia.

Put in clean litter and fresh bedding. Put fresh food into the dish. Place a fresh food store as near as possible to where you found the old one. Refill the water bottle and clip it on to the side of the cage.

Wash your hands thoroughly after cleaning out the cage and whenever you handle the hamster, especially before a meal.

Always wash your hands with soap and hot water after playing with your hamster or after cleaning its cage.

16

Do not try to play with your hamster during the day when it is resting or it will become bad-tempered. Only play with your hamster when it is ready for it – the best time is in the early evening.

Activity

Hamsters are nocturnal creatures. This means that they sleep during the day and are active at night. Do not disturb your hamster while it is sleeping. The best time to play with your hamster is in the evening, when it wakes up.

Wild hamsters hibernate (sleep) during the cold winter months. Sometimes a tame hamster will also start to hibernate. It will curl up with its legs tucked under its body and become quite stiff and cold.

If a hamster is left to sleep like this it will probably die. Warm a hibernating hamster gently in your hands or in a warm room, but do not try to bring it around too quickly.

A hamster will get plenty of exercise if you give it a wheel to play in. Give it some other toys to play with, too, such as as empty cotton spools, table-tennis balls or wood blocks.

Hamsters are very active animals and need plenty of exercise. Give your hamster plenty of toys such as an exercise wheel, a thick branch or an empty cotton spool, to keep it occupied.

Never give the hamster anything sharp or prickly which could damage the inside of its pouches, or anything with paint on it, as paint is poisonous to hamsters.

If you let your hamster run around on the floor, see that all the doors and windows are closed. Check that there are no small holes in the floor.

If you have a garden, let the hamster run beneath a special frame on the lawn. Take your hamster outside only if the weather is warm.

18

These pictures show you how to pick up a hamster. First hold the hamster by the back end of its body. When you have a firm hold, place the hamster on your other hand.

Handling

Although hamsters move very quickly, they do not have a good sense of height. Do not put them where they could fall and hurt themselves.

When you are used to holding your hamster, you can let it "run" from hand to hand.

Do not handle the hamster much at first. Give it time to settle into its new home. Start by stroking the hamster gently and offering scraps of food.

The photographs show the correct way to pick up a hamster. First cup two hands around the sides of its body. Close one hand over its back and curl your fingers and thumb gently, but firmly, around its body, with your wrist above its head. Lift the hamster quickly and place it on the upturned palm of your other hand.

19

Young hamsters are born about sixteen days after the mating. Clean the cage very carefully a few days before the litter is due, and put in extra hay for the female to build her nest.

Determining the sex of a hamster.

Male

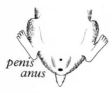

penis
anus

Female

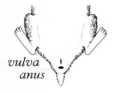

vulva
anus

The female's body is more tapered towards the rear. The female's genital opening is closer to the anus than the male's.

Breeding

Do not breed from your hamsters unless you can provide good homes for the young. Both the male and female must be in perfect health for breeding. Do not breed from the same family.

The best age for a first mating is five to six months. A female hamster is "in season" (ready to be mated) for four hours every four days – usually late at night – at any time of the year. If the female is in season, she will crouch very still with her back curved and her tail up.

If possible, mate the hamsters in a different cage from their own. If you do

20

Two-week-old hamsters. The young can stay with their mother for about three weeks until they are weaned (eating solid food). Separate the males from the females within twenty-eight days, for hamsters are able to mate when they are one month old.

not have a spare cage, put the female into the male's cage – never the other way around.

Watch the hamsters during mating as they may fight. You will have to separate them or they may injure each other. When you handle the hamsters, wear strong, thick gloves.

There are usually six to seven babies in a litter. Do not touch the young or disturb the nest or the mother for twenty-four hours. The young are born without hair and with their ears and eyes closed. Fur begins to grow after about a week. The eyes and ears begin to open during the second week.

A healthy hamster is one that is well fed and well looked after. If you are worried about your hamster's health, contact your vet immediately. After an illness the hamster's cage must be cleaned out and disinfected before it is used again.

Health and care

When you get your hamster, find out who your nearest vet is. If you think that your hamster is ill, contact the vet at once. Do not try to treat the hamster yourself.

Your hamster may be ill:
- if it lies in the cage without moving;
- if it does not eat;
- if its coat is dull, spiky or falling out;
- if it finds it hard to breathe, or the breathing is loud or uneven;
- if it has diarrhea or is constipated;
- if it is dragging its legs or finds it hard to move;
- if it is coughing or sneezing;
- if it has running eyes, nose or ears.

22

A hamster has teeth which keep growing. Usually they are worn down by eating and gnawing. Sometimes the teeth grow too long, especially when the hamster is old, and the hamster may have difficulty eating. If this happens, take the hamster to the vet, who will cut the teeth down.

The hamster's nails may also grow too long. These can be clipped by the vet, who may show your parents, or you, how to do this in the future.

Hamsters are very clean animals. They will groom themselves using their fore (front) feet. Proper feeding and care will help to keep the hamster's coat in good condition.

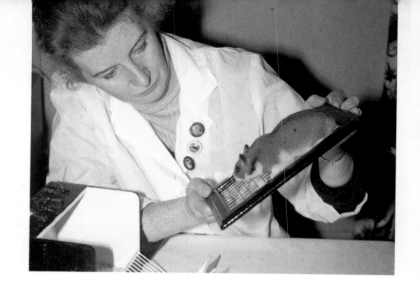

Shows

Some agricultural and livestock shows have sections where hamsters and other small animals can be exhibited. There are also hamster clubs and societies which organize special shows for their members.

There will be classes for standard breeds of hamsters, but there may be classes for pet hamsters too. Standard hamsters are judged on their shape, coat and eyes according to the standard set down for their breed. Pet hamsters are judged on their general condition and ease of handling.

If you want to show your hamster, you

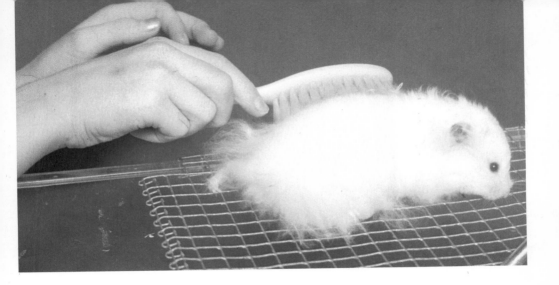

must start preparing for the show some weeks in advance.

At shows all hamsters are exhibited in special cages. You can buy these at a pet store. Give your hamster time to get used to being in the show cage.

You will also need a strong, well-ventilated wooden carrying box in which to put the show cage. These can be bought new or second hand, or be home made.

The owner of the winning hamster may get a card, rosette or trophy. Whether you win or not, shows are exciting places. You will also meet other people who share your interests.

Only long-haired hamsters need to be groomed regularly. Use a soft baby brush to brush the hamster's coat in the direction in which it grows – from head to tail. Before the show, stroke the hamster's coat the way it grows (from head to tail) with a piece of pure silk to bring out the shine.

If you leave your hamster with someone while you are away, tell the person what kind of food your pet likes to eat.
Your vet or local hamster breeder may know of someone who will take care of your pet for a small fee.

Going away

If you and your family go away and cannot take the hamster with you, remember to make arrangements for your pet. Perhaps you could ask friends to come into your house to feed and look after the hamster, or take it to their home.

Hamsters can be left without attention for two or three days if you make proper plans beforehand. Fix an extra water bottle to the cage, and leave enough dry food for the time that you will be away. Do not put fresh, wet or green food in the hamster's cage as this will go bad.

Cream hamster.

About hamsters

Hamsters are rodents. Rodents are animals with long, front teeth which are used for gnawing. Hamsters are related to other rodents such as rats, mice and gerbils.

Wild hamsters are found in the Middle East and parts of the desert regions of Russia and China. The pet hamster is descended from the Middle Eastern hamster.

The name hamster comes from the German word "hamstern", which means "to hoard". Hamsters collect their food, carry it in their pouches and then store or hoard it to eat later.

Lilac hamster photographed from behind to show its very short, stumpy tail.

Hamsters may be long- or short-haired. Although hamsters vary in size, the largest ones grow up to 15 cm (6 in) long from nose to tail. The female is larger than the male. Hamsters weigh between 100 and 150 gm ($3\frac{1}{2}$ and $5\frac{1}{4}$ oz).

Tame hamsters have much blunter faces than wild ones. Some hamsters have dark eyes. Others have red eyes.

The back legs are longer than the front ones. Hamsters use the front legs for putting food into their mouths and pouches. Hamsters look as if they do not have tails. In fact, they do have a very short tail.

There are more than thirty different

varieties of hamster in many beautiful
shades. The original hamster, the
golden, is a rich golden brown or tan
with some dark hairs on its back. It has
a flash of dark brown on each cheek
and a white underside to the body.

   Some varieties, called "selfs", are
the same shade all over. The selfs may
be cream, cinnamon, albino, white,
honey, yellow, fawn, gray, lilac, dove,
smoke, pearl or tortoiseshell.

   Other varieties are banded or spotted.
Banded hamsters have a white streak
along the sides of their bodies.

   Satin hamsters have a sheen on their
coat. Rex hamsters have very short,
plushy fur.

Above left
*Golden hamster –
the most
commonly-known
hamster.*

Above right
*Short-haired,
dark-eared
hamster.*

29

Checklist

Before you get your hamster you will need
- a food dish
- a gravity-flow water bottle
- litter (sawdust, peat, cat litter)
- bedding (hay, shredded vegetable parchment)
- enough food for the first week
- a container in which to carry the pet home

Each day
- Change the water
- Feed the hamster every evening
- Remove damp and soiled litter from cage
- Remove spoiled fresh food from the hoard
- Check that the hamster is lively and healthy

Each week
- Clean the cage completely
- Check that you have enough supplies of food, litter and bedding, and stock up if necessary

When necessary
- Prepare the hamster for showing
- Buy a show cage and carrying box

Glossary

Exercise wheel plastic wheel in which the hamster can play for exercise.

Gravity-flow water bottle small bottle with a long spout fixed upside down. The water flows out only when the hamster drinks.

Hibernating animals animals which go into a deep sleep during the cold winter months.

Litter absorbent material put on the floor of the cage to soak up dampness.

Litter the number of young born to the same mother at the same time.

Mash cereals or grain mixed together with a little water to make a crumbly mixture.

Mature fully-grown animal which is able to breed.

Nocturnal animal animal which sleeps during the day and is active at night.

Pouch loose, stretchy, skin in the cheeks of hamsters used for carrying food.

Weaning getting the young hamster used to eating solid food instead of suckling its mother's milk.

Index